A KiD'S MENSCH HANDBOOK

Step by Step to a Lifetime of Jewish Values

Teacher's Lesson Plan Manual
By Rachael Gelfman Schultz

24 Ready-to-Use Lesson Plans

Project Editor: Barbara D. Krasner
Design: Annemarie Redmond
Copyright © 2011 Behrman House, Inc.
Springfield, New Jersey
ISBN: 978-0-87441-932-0 • Manufactured in the United States of America

Behrman House, Inc.
www.behrmanhouse.com

Contents

Introduction 3
   Structure of the Textbook 3
   Structure of This Lesson Plan Manual 4

Lesson Plans

Part One: The Mensch Basics

Chapter 1	Welcome to A Kid's Mensch Handbook 8
	Lesson 1 8
Chapter 2	Making Mensch Choices 9
	Lesson 1 9
	Lesson 2 10
Chapter 3	Taking Mensch Actions 11
	Lesson 1 11
	Lesson 2 12
	Lesson 3 13

Part Two: Be a Mensch to Yourself

Chapter 4	Seeing Yourself as a Mensch 14
	Lesson 1 14
	Lesson 2 15
	Lesson 3 16
Chapter 5	Treating Yourself as a Mensch 17
	Lesson 1 17
	Lesson 2 18
	Lesson 3 19

Part Three: Be a Mensch to Others

Chapter 6	Ready, Set, Mensch! 20
	Lesson 1 20
	Lesson 2 21
	Lesson 3 22
Chapter 7	Be a Mensch to Your Family 23
	Lesson 1 23
	Lesson 2 24
	Lesson 3 25
Chapter 8	Be a Mensch to Your Friends and Classmates 26
	Lesson 1 26
	Lesson 2 27
	Lesson 3 28
Chapter 9	Be a Mensch to Everyone 29
	Lesson 1 29
	Lesson 2 30
	Lesson 3 31

Assessments 32

Introduction

A Kid's Mensch Handbook invites your students to explore timeless Jewish values in an accessible, modern, and exciting way. Through real-life examples, interactive activities, and a wealth of Jewish wisdom, *A Kid's Mensch Handbook* helps your students to make ethical choices, take positive actions, and treat all people—including themselves—with integrity and respect.

With *A Kid's Mensch Handbook*, you can provide your students with the knowledge and understanding to help foster Jewish values in their everyday lives. At the same time, the textbook will enrich your students' Jewish identity and connection to the Jewish community.

STRUCTURE OF THE TEXTBOOK

A Kid's Mensch Handbook is divided into three sections:

I. **The Mensch Basics** introduces the definition of a mensch: a good person, a person of integrity and respect. Each of us affects the world in profound ways; a mensch is someone who makes choices and takes action that affects the world in *positive* ways. Jewish sources, experience, and wisdom serve as guides to becoming menschen.

II. **Be a Mensch to Yourself** examines ways that introspection and self-examination can lead to self-respect and how self-respect can lead to respect for others. This section includes discussions of *b'tzelem Elohim*—the concept of being "created in God's image"—and *sh'mirat hab'riyut*—the mitzvah of caring for one's health.

III. **Be a Mensch to Others** explores ways to treat others with respect, generosity, and compassion. This section includes discussions of *talmud Torah*, "Jewish learning"; *sh'lom bayit*, "peace in the home"; *dibbuk ḥaverim*, "attachment to friends"; and *k'vod hab'riyot*, "respect for all people."

A Kid's Mensch Handbook also contains the following recurring features:

- **Mensch-Wise:** Thought-provoking questions to exercise skills in critical thinking.
- **Mensch Spotlight:** Profiles of role models from Jewish history to strengthen the link between the chapter and students' daily lives.
- **Top 5**: Short interactive activities based on the main topic of each chapter to help students apply Jewish values to their own lives.
- **Under the Mensch-ifying Glass:** Definitions of key Hebrew terms to clarify the meaning of core Jewish values.
- **A Note of Middot**: Explorations of *middot*—virtues—related to the chapter's main Jewish value to help students become menschen with timeless, practical advice.

Note: Izzy the Mensch-in-Training (the redhead cartoon character) appears throughout *A Kid's Mensch Handbook*, offering his wide-eyed commentary. Izzy's role is to amuse the students in the interest of enhancing their overall pleasure in the book and in Jewish learning. Allow students to giggle with him, give him funny voices, and enjoy watching him "grow up" as the book progresses.

STRUCTURE OF THIS LESSON PLAN MANUAL

This Lesson Plan Manual presents 24 ready-to-use lessons plans of approximately 50-60 minutes each for *A Kid's Mensch Handbook*. It includes suggestions for teaching every element of the student text. In addition, ideas on how to incorporate technology are included in this introduction and in many of the lesson plans.

Each chapter in this manual corresponds to a chapter in the textbook and includes one to three lesson plans that include:

- **Essential Question:** An overarching question, one that we may ask at different times in our lives that reflects the main idea of the lesson.
- **Lesson Objectives:** Specific goals for each lesson that correspond to the concepts and ideas that students should understand when they complete the lesson.
- **Getting Started**: A set induction to get students thinking about the ideas they will learn in that lesson.
- **Exploring the Text:** A step-by-step guide for presenting the lesson, including suggested questions and activities and the approximate time for each segment of the lesson.
- **Wrapping It Up:** A short activity or discussion to review and reflect on the main ideas presented in the lesson.

Note: *A Kid's Mensch Handbook* provides opportunities for your students to learn by sharing their opinions and personal experiences with one another. This Lesson Plan Manual contains open-ended questions to help you enhance this experience and keep the discussion focused and productive.

Experiential Learning

Each lesson plan also includes suggestions for experiential learning. Many students learn best by doing. As the ancient Chinese philosopher Confucius said: "Tell me and I will forget, show me and I may remember, involve me and I will understand." The activities suggested range from creating artwork, to performing a skit, to planning and executing *tzedakah* and volunteer projects. Whenever your class learns through direct experience, it is important for your students to reflect on their experience at the end of the activity or lesson. What did I learn from this activity? How does it deepen my understanding of the Jewish values we are studying? What questions does this experience raise for me?

Using This Lesson Plan Manual

At the start of the year, map out when you plan to teach each chapter. The 24 lessons in the manual have been designed so that you can teach an average of one lesson a week.

Before you begin to teach a textbook chapter, read through the Lesson Plan Manual to familiarize yourself with the chapter. You may choose to use the lessons exactly as they are, or you may adapt the lessons to fit the needs of your students. If you adapt the lessons, it is important to frame your lesson around an essential question—either the one suggested for the lesson or another one that points to the main idea of the lesson.

The Tech Connection

Your students are growing up in a world in which using technology is part of their daily lives at home and at school. There are infinite ways that you can take advantage of the Internet and digital applications to deepen understanding and to add creativity, interactivity, and excitement to your lessons. Many of the lesson plans include an activity labeled "The Tech Connection" that uses technology to explore the values in the text.

One way to take advantage of computer technology is to create a website or Wikispace devoted to *A Kid's Mensch Handbook*. If your congregation already has a website, find out if your class can have a space on it. Alternatively, there are instructions on the Internet for setting up your own website or Wikispace.

Use the class website or Wiki as an anchor activity throughout the year. An anchor activity is an ongoing project related to the curriculum that students can work on independently. Students might work on the website if they arrive early to school, are the first to finish a class assignment, or while you are working with another group of students. You might also designate class time when everyone works on projects that will be posted to the website.

The following suggestions will help you use technology in a variety of ways:

- Upload photographs of your students engaged in activities from the lesson plans in this manual or practicing the Jewish values discussed in this textbook.
- Post a survey question for parents based on a value in the chapter, then tally and share the results.
- Post students' responses to open-ended questions from the text or to **Essential Questions**.
- Set up a class blog. Students can write their reactions to class discussions.
- Conduct and write an interview with a mensch whom the students know personally. What did he or she do that makes him or her a mensch? What motivated him or her?
- Upload original artwork created by students depicting values in the chapter.
- Compile a list of volunteer opportunities in your community.
- Compile a list of potential *tzedakah* recipients, including Jewish and non-Jewish organizations that help Jews and non-Jews, especially organizations in which students are themselves involved.
- Compile a list of links to newspaper articles and websites documenting acts of real-life menschen.

At the beginning of the year, students can make a list of suggestions of ways they can use the Internet and their mobile devices to bring the material to life. Keep this list handy and implement their suggestions throughout the year.

Being Inclusive

Children vary in their learning styles. Some students learn best with a hands-on approach, while others do best with a visual or an auditory approach. In general, teachers who present material in many different ways will be able to reach many more children.

Teachers of children with special needs have extra challenges. These children may have a broad range of cognitive, physical, and behavioral disabilities that impact learning. It is always helpful to find out from parents what accommodations are made for their children in secular school. The suggestions included below are primarily for those children with learning, perceptual, or attention problems.

- For students with attention and auditory processing problems, teach in small increments and present one instruction at a time. Ask the children to repeat the instruction to be sure they have processed it.
- For children with attention problems, limit teaching segments to 10 to 15 minutes and allow for movement between activities.
- For children with decoding problems, make flash cards with a few key words. Children can take them home and practice reading them with their parents. Keep a shoe box of flash cards for children who need them. Provide opportunities for choral reading rather than asking children to read aloud individually.
- For children with attention and visual figure-ground problems, mask parts of the page so they can see only the section that is being worked on.
- For children with fine motor and handwriting problems, limit the amount of writing, drawing, and cutting that is required. The teacher or assistant may do difficult parts of a project and allow the student to finish the task.

Interpersonal and Intrapersonal Learners

Some students learn best through interacting with others (interpersonal); some learn best independently (intrapersonal). With this in mind, there are suggestions in the lesson plans for independent work and for activities and discussions with a partner, group, or the whole class. In general, if the manual does not specify that students are meeting with a partner or in a group, plan to have a class discussion.

Group Work

Many of the lessons include suggestions for group work. Whenever possible, plan ahead how you want to form the groups. It is important to change the composition of your groups. For some tasks you will want students with a variety of talents and interests. For others you may choose to group together students with similar skills.

Group work is most successful when every group member knows his or her responsibilities. To help make the group's task clear, prepare written instructions before the class. Many of the lesson plans include such instructions.

Being Menschen in the Classroom
Here are some ways you can encourage your students to be menschen in the classroom:

- *Foster a sense of security and fellowship.* Make it clear that your classroom is a safe space where students will be heard with respect and be guided, not judged. When a student prefers not to share, please respect his or her privacy.
- *Be aware.* Your students will come to class from a variety of backgrounds and experiences. Some students will have the maturity to manage emotions well; others will not. Teach all of your students to see Jewish values as a supportive guide to making life's tough decisions.
- *Be a role model.* Most importantly, remember that the interpersonal relationships you build and the tone and atmosphere you create in your classroom are as important as the material you teach. At all times, try to model and encourage the qualities of patience and tolerance in all of your students. Show your students what it means to be a mensch!

Scope and Sequence
Each chapter of *A Kid's Mensch Handbook* examines a core concept that serves as the chapter's main theme:

Chapter	Pages	Core Concept
1	8–13	Each of us affects the world in profound ways. A mensch is someone who takes action that is generous and kind, action that affects the world in *positive* ways.
2	14–23	It is important to make good, ethical choices. Jewish sources, experience, and wisdom can help us to determine and make good choices.
3	24–35	Once we've made good choices, we must take action. An important guide to taking "mensch action" is The Golden Rule—*v'ahavta l'reacha kamocha*—love your neighbor as yourself.
4	38–49	We respect ourselves because we are created *b'tzelem Elohim*—in God's image. When we understand how it feels to respect *ourselves*, we better understand how *others* feel when we respect them.
5	50–61	We exercise self-respect through *sh'mirat hab'riyut*—guarding one's health. By caring for our bodies and our minds, we better prepare ourselves to be menschen to others.
6	64–75	A good way to learn how to treat others respectfully is through *talmud Torah*—Jewish learning. *Talmud Torah* may be the most important mitzvah of all, because learning leads to action.
7	76–87	We practice treating others respectfully with the value of *sh'lom bayit*—peace in the home.
8	88–99	We learn to treat friends and classmates respectfully with the value of *dibbuk ḥaverim*—attachment to friends.
9	100–111	We can show respect for all people through the values of *k'vod hab'riyot*—respect for all people; *derech eretz*—good manners; *k'lal Yisrael*—support for the world Jewish community; and *tzedakah*—righteousness.
Special Sections	112–118	We can review what we've learned with "Mensch Magic," "Mensch Sections Diploma," and the "Handy-Dandy Mensch Index."

Welcome to a Kid's Mensch Handbook Lesson 1
Essential Question: What does it mean to be a mensch?

Lesson Objectives: Students will be able to:
1. Describe how our actions "ripple out" and affect others.
2. Define "mensch" and articulate qualities that characterize a mensch.
3. Identify menschen in their own lives and famous menschen, and explain what makes them menschen.

Getting Started: (5 minutes)
Students brainstorm a list of qualities that describe a good person. Write the list on the board. If your students need some help getting started, start the exercise by writing *kindness*, *honesty*, and *respect*. Leave the list on the board for the rest of the class.

Exploring the Text:
1. (5 minutes) Give each student a copy of *A Kid's Mensch Handbook.* Student volunteers read **Making Waves** (pages 9–10). Ask: "What are some examples of actions that affect others?" Students may share examples of the ways they have affected others positively and explain what they learned from the experience.
2. (5 minutes) Students read the first paragraph of **That's Fine and Dandy** (page 10) aloud. Students can alternate reading the bulleted items and then add definitions of their own, based on their brainstorming on the board.
3. (10 minutes) Each student completes **Too Many to Menschen** (page 11), and then shares his or her answers with a partner.

Experiential Learning: (10 minutes)
Each student chooses one of their three menschen from **Too Many to Menschen** (page 11), and makes a collage (using a computer or magazines, newspapers, markers, etc. that you provide), writes a poem, draws a picture, or chooses another form of artistic expression to explain what makes this person a mensch. When the students are done, they can walk around the room and look at each other's artwork.

The Tech Connection: (5 minutes)
While preparing their artwork, students search the Internet to find out more about their mensch's life or find images that express what makes that person a mensch. You can post the students' digital artwork on the class website, or photograph artwork and post it.

> **Wrapping It Up:** (10 minutes)
> Write on the board: "The great rabbi Hillel said: 'If I am not for myself, who will be for me? If I am only for myself, what am I? And if not now, when?'" As a class, discuss what Hillel means. How is Hillel asking us to act toward ourselves and others? What does Hillel's saying have to do with being a mensch? Read pages 12-13 together and explain the basic structure of the book.

Making Mensch Choices Lesson 1
Essential Question: How do our choices affect ourselves and others?

Lesson Objectives: Students will be able to:
1. Describe how their choices affect themselves and others.
2. Explain how good choices are more likely to have a positive outcome.
3. Identify factors that can get in the way of making good choices.

Getting Started: (10 minutes)
Each student recalls the hardest choice he or she ever had to make. (Explain that these should be ethical dilemmas, not preferences, like the choice between vanilla and chocolate.) Ask:
- What made the choice so difficult?
- Were you pleased with the outcome?
- If presented with the same situation now, would you make the same choice?

Students share their tough choices with the class.

Exploring the Text:
1. (5 minutes) Explain that the class will now work through a tough choice *together.* A volunteer reads **The New-Kid Dilemma, Part 1** (page 15) aloud. Each student answers the question, in writing, at the bottom of the page: What would *you* choose to do? Encourage students to think in terms of good choices, as opposed to what others might think.

2. **Experiential Learning:** (15 minutes) Divide the students into groups of four to make skits of **The New-Kid Choice Dilemma**. In each group, one student plays Alex, and the other three play the kids at the table. Each group performs one of the following scenarios: (*The skit should include what the students imagine will be the results of your choice and Alex's.*)
    a) You and your friends ask Alex to join you, and Alex says no.
    b) You and your friends ask Alex to join you, Alex says yes and moves to your table.
    c) You do nothing, and Alex continues to eat alone.

3. (5 minutes) Students work individually to complete **The New Kid-Choice Chart** exercise (page 16). (*Obviously, choice A leads to the more positive results.*) Bring the students together and discuss: What would you do in this situation? What do you think is the best choice? How do you know it is the best choice? What might motivate someone to make a bad choice in this situation? Point out that making good choices does not always lead to a positive result, but making bad choices almost never does.

4. (10 minutes) Each student completes **Three Cheers, Three Jeers** (page 18) and shares his or her answers with a partner.

Wrapping It Up: (5 minutes)
Bring the students together and ask: "What makes a good choice? What makes a not-so-good choice? How do our choices affect ourselves and others? Why do we not always make good choices?" (*Peer pressure, anger, jealousy.*)

Making Mensch Choices Lesson 2
Essential Question: How do we make good choices?

Lesson Objectives: Students will be able to:
1. Describe and evaluate the different ways we make choices.
2. Define Tanach, Talmud, *midrashim*, and *hachnasat or'ḥim*.
3. Explain how the Tanach, Talmud, and *midrashim* can provide valuable guidance today, just as they did for our ancestors.

Getting Started: (5 minutes)
Ask: "Have you ever learned something important from a story that your parents or grandparents told you?" The story may be about what happened to them, or to their parents or grandparents, or even to someone in Jewish history. What did they learn? Students share with the class.

Exploring the Text:
1. (5 minutes) Student volunteers read **The Choice Is Yours** (page 17) aloud. Discuss: What do you have in common with people who lived hundreds of years ago and with those who will live hundreds of years from now? Can the good choices of earlier generations help us? How?

2. **Experiential Learning:** (10 minutes) All the students stand up. Give the students several dilemmas. Students go to one side of the room if they think the answer is yes, and go to the other side of the room if they think the answer is no. Representatives from each side of the room share their reasoning. Then students may switch sides if they are convinced of the other side's argument. Choose from the **dilemmas** in the middle of page 17 and the top of page 19. Ask: "How did you make these choices? What kinds of different things did you consider? Is there one 'right' choice?" Then read **Good Choice!** (pages 19–20) aloud.

3. (5 minutes) Explain that, just like in your family, the Jewish "family" tells many stories of our past to help us learn how to make better choices, and these stories can be found in the Tanach, Talmud, and *midrashim*. Read **Torah, Talmud, and Beyond** (page 21) together.

4. **The Tech Connection:** (5 minutes) Start a glossary on the class website, including Tanach, Talmud, *midrashim*, and *hachnasat or'ḥim*.

5. (5 minutes) Read **The New-Kid Dilemma, Part 2** (page 22) together, and complete **You're Welcome!** at the bottom of the page. Invite students to share their answers. Discuss: In what ways can *you* welcome guests and strangers at your school?

6. (10 minutes) Students read the **Yiddish proverbs** (page 23) and provide an example of how each of the proverbs teaches them to make good choices. For example, "Too much of anything is unhealthy" reminds us not to overindulge—in TV, or food, or sleep.

Wrapping It Up: (5 minutes)
Each student writes one concrete thing he or she would like to do better based on what we have learned today from earlier generations of Jews—either from the story about Abraham and Sarah and their *hachnasat or'ḥim*, or from the Yiddish proverbs. Students who wish to can share with the class.

Taking Mensch Actions, Lesson 1
Essential Question: Why is it important to follow good choices with positive action?

Lesson Objectives: Students will be able to:
1. Discuss why it is important to follow good choices with positive action.
2. Define *mitzvot* and understand why they are important.
3. Provide several examples of *mitzvot*.

Getting Started: (5 minutes)
Student volunteers act out the following two scenes:
1. Student A drops a pencil on the floor. Student B *chooses* to pick up the pencil for Student A, but takes no action. (Tell Student B to wish very, very hard.)
2. Student A drops a pencil on the floor. Student B chooses to pick up the pencil, then actually picks it up and gives it to Student A.

Discuss:
- What was the difference between the two scenes?
- Was Student B in the first scene a mensch? *(We don't know; he or she didn't do anything.)*
- What does this exercise teach us about being a mensch? *(In order to be a mensch, we must take action.)*

Exploring the Text:
1. (10 minutes) Divide the students into groups of four. Each group reads the **dialogue** on pages 25 and 26 as a short play. Assign students the parts of Rachel, her big brother, her grandmother, and the narrator. After they read the play, each group answers the following questions:
    - What is the difference between Rachel and her grandmother's approaches?
    - Whose approach do you think is better? Why? Encourage your students to think in terms of which approach leads to *action*.
2. (10 minutes) Students complete **The Mitzvah Marvel** (page 23) individually. Students share their answers with the class. Ask: "What opportunities for *mitzvot* have you had today?"
3. (5 minutes) Read **Mitzvah Your Way to Mensch-hood** (page 28). Point to the photo of the boy at summer camp on page 28. A volunteer reads the caption aloud. Ask: "What are some other opportunities to perform *mitzvot* at summer camp?" *(Answers may include: cleaning the bunk, being kind to our campmates, sticking up for kids who are being picked on.)* Explain that wherever we may be, there are opportunities to perform *mitzvot*.
4. **Experiential Learning:** (15 minutes) Like Rachel and her grandmother, each student decorates a *tzedakah* box to bring home so that he or she can do the mitzvah of *tzedakah*, transforming mensch choices into action.
5. **The Tech Connection:** (5 minutes) Add mitzvah, *rodef shalom*, *tzedakah*, *l'shon hara*, and *bikkur ḥolim* to the glossary on the class website. Students can find images on the Internet to illustrate these *mitzvot*.

Wrapping It Up: (5 minutes)
Students read **Quick Quote** (page 26) aloud. Ask: "How is wisdom without action like a tree without fruit?" *(We cannot benefit from it unless it is something we see, feel, experience, etc.)* Students think of other analogies by finishing the sentence: Wisdom without action is like _____.

Taking Mensch Actions, Lesson 2
Essential Question: What are the mitzvah opportunities in our own lives?

Lesson Objectives: Students will be able to:
1. Identify mitzvah opportunities in their own lives.
2. Distinguish between ritual and ethical *mitzvot*.
3. Describe what Naḥshon ben Aminadav did and explain why he is a mensch.

Getting Started: (10 minutes)
Write a typical student schedule on the board, including wake up and get ready, class, lunch, recess, return home, homework, dinner, free time, bed time, etc. Go through the schedule in order, and have students list *mitzvot* that can be performed during each time slot. Write the *mitzvot* on the board, next to each time slot. Explain that *mitzvot* can be anything that helps yourself or others, from brushing your teeth, to praying, to being nice to your little sister.

Exploring the Text:
1. (5 minutes) Read **Mitzvah Twins** (page 28). Students categorize the *mitzvot* on the board as ritual or ethical. Write an "R" next to ritual *mitzvot* and an "E" next to ethical *mitzvot*.
2. (5 minutes) Students complete **A Mitzvah a Day** (page 29). Hand out Post-its®. Students write down the *mitzvot* they would like to add to their routine on the Post-it, and put it somewhere they see every day (*inside their assignment notebook, pencil case, etc.*) Volunteers share what they wrote on the Post-it note.
3. (5 minutes) Read the **last paragraph** on page 29 together. Brainstorm *mitzvot* that can be done once in a while. Discuss: What clues does my mensch radar pick up to help me recognize a mitzvah opportunity? (*A new student comes to school, my friend looks sad, I see a homeless person on the street.*)
4. (5 minutes) Complete **Mitzvah Calendar** (page 30) and discuss the question at the bottom. Ask: "Are there *mitzvot* you do once in a while that you would like to do more often?"
5. **Experiential Learning:** (10 minutes) Read **Scene** (page 31) together. Students write a paragraph or poem from the perspective of an Israelite at the Sea of Reeds who is scared to move forward. Then read **Action** (page 31) together. Write another paragraph or poem from Naḥshon's perspective. Discuss: What made Naḥshon a mensch?
6. (10 minutes) Students write a paragraph about a time when they overcame doubts or difficulties to take action, even when no one else did. Volunteers share with the class.

Wrapping It Up: (5 minutes)
Discuss: Why do we sometimes fail to see mitzvah opportunities, or see mitzvah opportunities and not act? How can we get better at seeing the mitzvah opportunities in our own lives and acting on them?

Taking Mensch Actions, Lesson 3
Essential Question: Why is "love your neighbor as yourself" one of the most important *mitzvot*?

Lesson Objectives: Students will be able to:
1. Understand the meaning of The Golden Rule and how it leads to all other *mitzvot*.
2. Give examples of loving your neighbor as yourself.
3. Explain what *middot* are and why they are important.

Getting Started: (5 minutes)
Students stand up. Explain that after you count to three, they all will stand on one foot, and say the entire Torah (whatever is most important in Judaism) out loud while still standing on one foot. Give them a moment to think of what they will say, and then they all stand on one foot and talk at once. Ask: "What did you say? What is the most important part (or parts) of the Torah—and Judaism as a whole? Why?"

Exploring the Text:
1. (5 minutes) Read **The All-in-One Mitzvah** (page 32) together. Remind the students of the **mitzvot** you discussed last class. Ask about each mitzvah: "Does this help you to love your neighbor as yourself?" (*The answer to most—or all—should be yes.*)
2. (5 minutes) Explain that starting here, every chapter will contain a Jewish value in Hebrew, including an **Under the Mensch-ifying Glass** discussion of the Hebrew words themselves. Then read page 33 and **Falling into Place** (page 34).
3. **Experiential Learning:** (10 minutes) Each student writes down a memory, creates a (very) short story or poem, draws a picture, or finds an image or short story online in which someone fulfills the mitzvah of "love your neighbor as yourself."
4. **The Tech Connection:** (5 minutes) Create a new part of the class website called "Under the Mensch-ifying Glass" that includes the Jewish value in Hebrew, the explanation of the Hebrew words from the textbook, and the student's illustrations from the above exercise.
5. (5 minutes) Students complete **One More Time** (page 34) and share with a partner.
6. (5 minutes) A student volunteer reads **A Note of Middot** (page 35). To demonstrate how *middot* work, student volunteers say "I'm sorry" in two ways: (1) as a genuine apology; and (2) a sarcastic "Sor-*ree*." Ask: "What is the difference between the two? Which kind helps make someone a mensch?"
7. (5 minutes) Student volunteers read **Generosity** (page 35). Ask: "Why is *leiv tov* important in the classroom? At home? In the community?" Encourage them to think of instances—when we are upset, or sick, or hungry—when we rely on one another's generosity.

Wrapping It Up: (5 minutes)
Students write down one new thing that they would like to do in the next week to fulfill "love your neighbor as yourself."

Seeing Yourself as a Mensch, Lesson 1

Essential Question: How can we examine ourselves and challenge ourselves to take positive actions?

Lesson Objectives: Students will be able to:
1. Discuss why it is important to examine our choices and actions.
2. Describe what it means to treat ourselves with respect.
3. Explain how respecting ourselves impacts the way we relate to others.

Getting Started: (5 minutes)
Students make a list of words or phrases that describe people who respect themselves. Write the list on the board. Begin the list with the word *mensch*. Leave the list on the board for the remainder of the lesson.

Exploring the Text:
1. (5 minutes) Students read **The Mensch-Cam** (page 39) together. Ask:
   - What does it mean to be "the hero—and the author—of your life story"? *(We can choose our own actions, which in turn affect those around us.)*
   - Why is it important to examine our actions? *(To make sure that we make good choices and take positive actions—mensch actions.)*
2. (10 minutes) Students complete **Mensch Movie Review** (page 40). Students choose one scene to share with a partner and discuss their answers to the last question.
3. **Experiential Learning:** (15 minutes) Give each student a blank piece of white paper with the outline of a face on it. Each student creates a self-portrait through making a collage (using images from the computer or from newspapers or magazines) inside the outline. Explain that you are not necessarily trying to represent what you actually look like, but to represent things that you see as important about yourself.
4. (5 minutes) Divide the students into small groups. Each student in the group shares his or her artwork and answers the question: What did you learn from doing this exercise about how you see yourself?
5. (5 minutes) Write the **quote from *Pirkei Avot*** (page 41) on the board: "Know what is above you. An eye that sees and an ear that hears." Ask: "Whose eyes and ears are we talking about? Would it change the way you act if you always imagined God watching everything you say and do? How?"

Wrapping It Up: (5 minutes)
Discuss: Does how you see yourself matter? Does it change how you act? Does it make a difference whether you respect yourself? Why? Read **I Know What You Mean** (page 41) together.

Seeing Yourself as a Mensch, Lesson 2
Essential Question: What does it mean to be created in the image of God?

Lesson Objectives: Students will be able to:
1. Understand what it means to be created *b'tzelem Elohim*—in the image of God.
2. Provide concrete examples of acting in God's image.
3. Explain the connection between being created in God's image and being "happy with one's lot."

Getting Started: (5 minutes)
Ask: "What words would you use to describe God?" Write the words on the board.

Exploring the Text:
1. (10 minutes) Read together the passage from the Torah where the phrase first appears: "And God created the human in God's image…male and female God created them. And God blessed them and said to them, 'Be fruitful and multiply and fill the earth.…'" (Genesis 1:27–28). Why does the Torah tell us that we were created in God's image? What is the Torah trying to teach us? Then read **In God's Image** (page 42) together.

2. (5 minutes) Students complete the sentence, "Like God, we…" Write the different sentences on the board. If students are stuck, read **The Breath of Life** (page 43) first and then add their own sentences. Alternatively, read page 43 after the students make their own sentences.

3. (5 minutes) In pairs, students share a time when they were like God. (*Examples may include reciting blessings over Shabbat candles; writing a story or painting a picture; standing up for a younger sibling.*)

4. **The Tech Connection:** (5 minutes) Add *b'tzelem Elohim* to the class website with illustrations of people acting in God's image.

5. **Experiential Learning:** (10 minutes) Read **Two Pockets** (page 44) together. Several students volunteer to come up to the front of the room to perform some "improv." Give each student a note to put in his or her pocket that no one else sees. Some students receive a note that says, "For me the world was created," others receive a note that says, "I am but dust and ashes," and one person receives two notes, one of each. The audience suggests a scene (*a Little League game, the school bus, science class*) and the students each act according to their notes. The audience guesses who has which note (or notes) and explains how they figured it out. The student actors explain why they acted as they did.

6. (10 minutes) Read **A Note of Middot** (page 49) together. Ask: "What are you grateful for?" Focus on blessings that are not material, such as family, friends, and health. Each student makes a list. Students may put their lists inside of their *siddurim* on the page of the Amidah that says *Modim Anaḥnu Lah*, where we thank God for the blessings in our lives.

Wrapping It Up: (5 minutes)
Each student writes down one new thing he or she would like to do in order to be like God. Volunteers share with the class.

Seeing Yourself as a Mensch, Lesson 3
Essential Question: How can we practice self-respect in our own lives?

Lesson Objectives: Students will be able to:
1. Provide examples of ways to practice self-respect.
2. Explain how personal reflection and prayer can help build self-respect.
3. Understand why we can only respect ourselves when we are true to ourselves.

Getting Started: (5 minutes)
Students complete the following sentence: "I respect myself the most when I _____." Volunteers share their sentences with the class.

Exploring the Text:
1. (2 minutes) Explain that each of the next five chapters will include a **Top 5** list, with ideas, suggestions, and tips for bringing that chapter's Jewish value to life.
2. (8 minutes) Students complete **Take Stock** (page 45) and share one of their answers with a partner. Explain that there are no right or wrong answers to this *b'tzelem Elohim* quiz. The objective is to be honest with yourself in order to evaluate your actions.
3. (10 minutes) Divide the students into three groups. Each group reads **Be Kind** (page 46) together and writes a list of ways in which we can show more kindness and compassion. Group One focuses on "in school," Group Two "at home," and Group Three "by yourself." Each group presents to the class. Then each student writes down one way he or she wants to show more kindness in each of the three categories.
4. (10 minutes) Read **Be Yourself** (page 47) as a class. Ask: "What does the question mean, 'Reb Zusya, why were you not like Zusya?' What does this story ask each one of us to do?" Remind your students that according to Jewish belief, each person was born for a special purpose. Rather than trying to be someone else, we should each be the best person we can be. Answer the **question** at the bottom of the page individually. Volunteers share their answers.
5. **Experiential Learning:** (10 minutes) Hand out blank pieces of paper to each student for **Recharge Your Batteries** (page 48). If your students ask for more guidance, encourage them to draw or write about a favorite place, book, or memory. When they are done, the students can walk around the room and look at each others' artwork.

> **Wrapping It Up:** (5 minutes)
> Read **Speak with God** (page 48) together. Encourage students to think of prayer services in a different way—as an opportunity to reflect on their day and their week, and to think of ways they can be even more of a mensch. Each student writes a short personal prayer reflecting on ways he or she can become more of a mensch—someone who acts with self-respect and in God's image.

A Kid's Mensch Handbook • Teacher's Lesson Plan Manual

Treating Yourself as a Mensch, Lesson 1
Essential Question: Why is it a mitzvah to treat our bodies with respect?

Lesson Objectives: Students will be able to:
1. Discuss why it is important to treat our bodies with respect.
2. Explain how being created in the image of God obligates us to take care of our bodies.
3. Understand the connection between treating our bodies with respect and being a mensch.

Getting Started: (10 minutes)
Divide the class into groups of three or four students. Write the following quote from Maimonides on the board: "The body is the instrument of the soul." Ask: "What do you think this quote means? In what ways is the body the 'instrument of the soul'?" Give the groups 5 minutes to discuss their answers. Then each group presents its conclusion to the class. Explain that this chapter will discuss the importance of treating our bodies—and our minds—with respect.

Exploring the Text:
1. (10 minutes) Read **Squeaky Brakes** (page 51) together. Then repeat the story, but this time the students stand up each time the narrator makes a bad choice. Each time a student stands up, ask him or her to say what he or she would have done differently. At the end of the story, discuss: How is taking care of a bicycle like taking care of your body? (*Both require care, maintenance, and attention.*)

2. (5 minutes) In pairs, complete **Dr. Goodmensch** (page 52). For each Rx pad, encourage students to think of specific ways to help each patient—perhaps by joining a sports team, paying attention in class, or eating an apple a day.

3. (5 minutes) Two volunteers act out the exchange between Hillel and his student in **Hillel's Mitzvah** (page 53). (*The student reads the first paragraph, Hillel the second, then they alternate.*) Ask: "Why is it more important to care for our bodies than for a statue?" (*Answers may include: A statue does not require care to live; we are created in God's image, while a statue is not; caring for ourselves is a mitzvah.*)

4. **Experiential Learning:** (15 minutes) Look at the **photo** (page 53) together. Ask: "What are some of your favorite healthful foods?" Together, make a class cookbook of healthy foods. Each student writes and illustrates one recipe to submit to the cookbook. (*A recipe can be simple, such as spread peanut-butter on celery and put raisins on top.*)

5. **The Tech Connection:** (10 minutes) Students search online for recipes and images. Post the cookbook to the class website.

Wrapping It Up: (5 minutes)
Read **A Lifelong Loan** (page 53). Ask: "Do you treat something you borrow differently than something you own? How? How should we treat our body if it's a loan to us? Why?"

Treating Yourself as a Mensch, Lesson 2
Essential Question: What is the mitzvah of *sh'mirat hab'riyut*?

Lesson Objectives: Students will be able to:
1. Define *sh'mirat hab'riyut*.
2. Understand how the body and mind work together and affect each other.
3. Describe what Yael Arad did and explain why she is a mensch.

Getting Started: (5 minutes)
Ask: "How do you feel when you do not get a good night's sleep? Or when you forget to eat breakfast? Or when you eat too many potato chips? How do you feel when you get a good night's sleep? Or after a good healthy meal? How does taking care of your body affect how you feel?"

Exploring the Text:
1. (2 minutes) Read **Be a Body Mensch** (page 54) together. Suggest beginning a new class tradition—when someone sneezes, the rest of the class says, "*Lab'riyut!*"
2. **The Tech Connection:** (5 minutes) Add *sh'mirat hab'riyut* to the class website with illustrations of people taking care of their bodies.
3. (5 minutes) Read **Mensch-Wise** (page 54) together. Ask: "Should body piercing be permitted?" Students make arguments in favor and against. Then the class votes.
4. (10 minutes) Illustrate the close relationship between our bodies and minds with the following scenarios:
    a) It's one hour before bedtime. You've got a big test tomorrow, and your spelling is still rusty. But you're having so much fun playing your newest video game. What do you do?
    b) You've just come home from religious school, and you're *really* hungry. Dinner will be ready in half an hour, but the cookie jar is full—and no one's looking.
   Ask students to describe the results of each possible action, and how the actions will affect their bodies. Then read **All in the Mind** (page 55) together.
5. **Experiential Learning:** (5 minutes) Students stand up and do ten jumping jacks. Ask: "Do you feel differently now than you felt before you did the jumping jacks? How? How does exercise affect your energy level and feelings?"
6. (5 minutes) Have students complete **Body-ography** (page 56) individually.
7. (8 minutes) Read **Mensch Spotlight** (page 57) together. Students describe how *sh'mirat hab'riyut* helped Yael Arad to be a mensch to herself and to others. (*Because Yael Arad showed respect for her body, she was able to bring happiness and pride to her country.*) Ask: "Is there a famous athlete who you think is a mensch? Who? Why?"

Wrapping It Up: (5 minutes)
Students share their **Looking Ahead** resolutions from **Body-ography** (page 57). Challenge your students to fulfill their resolutions in the coming week.

Treating Yourself as a Mensch, Lesson 3
Essential Question: How can we practice *sh'mirat hab'riyut* in our own lives?

Lesson Objectives: Students will be able to:
1. Provide concrete examples of how to practice *sh'mirat hab'riyut* in our lives.
2. Understand how self-discipline influences our choices and behavior.
3. Make healthful choices based on Jewish wisdom and experience.

Getting Started: (5 minutes)
Students brainstorm a list of guidelines for treating their bodies with respect. Write the guidelines on the board.

Exploring the Text:
1. (5 minutes) Ask: "Why do you think the Talmud forbids Jews to live in a city that does not contain a vegetable garden?" *(Answers may include: Because we should always have access to healthful food; because gardens provide food year after year; because gardens teach us to work together and share responsibility.)* Then complete **Eat Mensch Food** (page 58) individually.

2. (5 minutes) Each student completes **Get Movin'** (page 59) individually. Explain to your students that the yellow face in the middle has a "neutral" expression, to be used for activities that the student considers so-so. For fun, take a poll to determine the class's favorite activities.

3. (5 minutes) Read **Sleep Tight** (page 59) together. Ask: "Do you think Jewish law considers depriving a neighbor of sleep stealing?" *(Answers may include: Sleep is valuable; Jewish law considers our health very important.)* Ask: "What changes (if any) do you need to make in your routine to ensure that you get enough sleep?"

4. (10 minutes) Complete **Be a Danger Dodger** (page 60) individually. Explain that "don't rely on a miracle" means that each of us is responsible for thinking ahead. Students share their answers with a partner.

5. (5 minutes) Read **Balance Yourself** (page 60) together. Show the students the entire blessing, in Hebrew and English, in the *siddur*. Explain that the blessing is said after going to the bathroom. Ask: "Why do we bless God after going to the bathroom?"

6. **Experiential Learning:** (10 minutes) Divide the students into at least two groups. Each group reads **A Note of Middot** (page 61) together. Then each group creates and performs a skit in which a person goes through a typical day in the students' life, including waking up, going to school, taking part in extracurricular activities, and coming home, with a voice-over describing the person's thought processes. In Group One's skit, the hero of the skit has excellent self-discipline. In Group Two's skit, the hero has no self-discipline. Discuss the difference.

Wrapping It Up: (5 minutes)
Ask: "How does making healthy choices and respecting our bodies make a difference in our lives?" Each student states one word to describe someone who respects his body *(happy, healthy, energized, mensch)*.

Ready, Set, Mensch! Lesson 1

Essential Question: How is learning essential to our lives and the life of the Jewish people?

Lesson Objectives: Students will be able to:
1. Understand how learning helps us become menschen.
2. Discuss how the Torah has helped to unify and strengthen the Jewish people.
3. Describe how Rabbi Akiva continued to learn Torah despite the Roman decree and explain why Rabbi Akiva is a mensch.

Getting Started: (5 minutes)
Students share with the class a time when they learned something new. Ask:
- Why is it important to begin with small steps and to practice? *(So we can become better and better.)*
- Why is this lesson important as we learn to become menschen? *(We must learn how to be menschen to others, then become better and better.)*

Read **First Things First** (page 65) together.

Exploring the Text:
1. (10 minutes) Each student completes **The Tree of Knowledge** (page 66) and shares his or her answers with a partner.
2. (5 minutes) Ask: "Today, the Jewish people lives all over the world, from Alaska to India. What keeps the Jewish people together, when we live in so many different places and lead such different lives? *(Answers may include: Israel, prayers, Torah.)* Read **Learning to the Rescue** (page 67) together.
3. **Experiential Learning:** (12 minutes) Draw an outline of a tree on a big poster board. Tell your students: "The Torah is often referred to as *Etz Ḥayim,* the Tree of Life, because it provides nourishment and sustenance for the Jewish people." Hand out one piece of construction paper to each student. Each piece of paper is shaped like a leaf or fruit. Ask: "What are some ways the Torah provides nourishment for the Jewish people? Each student writes an answer on his or her piece of paper with an illustration. *(Answers may include: Its laws teach us how to live our lives; it connects us to God; it provides us with wisdom and guidance.)* Collect the responses and glue them on the tree. You may leave the poster board up as a decoration for the classroom that reminds the students of the importance of the Torah to the Jewish people.
4. (8 minutes) Read about **Rabbi Akiva** on page 68. Ask: "What do *you* have in common with Rabbi Akiva?" Students talk about times when they did the right thing though it may have been unpopular. What did they learn from the experience?
5. (5 minutes) Read **A Note of Middot** (page 75) together. Ask: "How does it make you feel when someone brags about his or her grades?"

Wrapping It Up: (5 minutes)
A student volunteer reads **Quick Quote** (page 67) aloud. Ask: "How does learning help the Jewish people survive? What would happen if we didn't learn?"

Ready, Set, Mensch! Lesson 2
Essential Question: Why is the mitzvah of *talmud Torah* one of the most important *mitzvot*?

Lesson Objectives: Students will be able to:
1. Define *talmud Torah*.
2. Explain why Jewish tradition considers *talmud Torah* the most important mitzvah.
3. Describe how *talmud Torah* leads to action.

Getting Started: (3 minutes)
Ask: "What is the most important mitzvah? Why?"

Exploring the Text:
1. (7 minutes) Read **The Most Important Mitzvah** (page 69) together. To eliminate confusion, explain that the Talmud is an important set of books that contain Jewish law; the Hebrew word *talmud* means "learning." *Talmud Torah* refers to Jewish learning in general, not the set of books.

    Divide the class into groups of two or three. On the board, write: Hebrew, Jewish history, and Israel. Students list as many Jewish subjects as they can in two minutes. A representative from each group shares the group's list with the class. Write the subjects on the board. If students don't name them, be sure to include: Jewish holidays, Jewish values, and of course, Torah. Explain that even learning about our families and our heritage may be considered *talmud Torah*.

2. **The Tech Connection:** (5 minutes) Add *talmud Torah* to the class website together with illustrations of different Jewish subjects.

3. (5 minutes) In pairs, students debate which is more important, learning or action. One student in each pair is assigned each side of the debate. Read **The Great Debate** (page 70) together.

4. (5 minutes) Have students complete **Mensch-Wise** (page 70) individually.

5. (5 minutes) In the same pairs as above, complete **Mount Mitzvah** (page 71). Point out that students should begin the exercise from the bottom, then "climb" the mountain by connecting the three levels.

6. **Experiential Learning**: (15 minutes) Years ago, when children began religious school, they received a little chalkboard with the letters of the *alef-bet* on it—covered with honey. As they recited each letter, they were allowed to "taste" the sweetness of learning. This ceremony was usually followed by treats of honey cake, apples, and nuts. Use this story as a springboard to hold a celebration of the chapter's lesson. If possible, invite your students' families to come to class. Bring everyone to the synagogue library. Encourage them to borrow a book, video, or musical recording, and to browse through the Jewish newspapers and magazines. Make the occasion festive. You and your class can bring in sweet treats to emphasize the sweetness of *talmud Torah*. Perhaps invite your cantor or music director to teach some Israeli music.

Wrapping It Up: (5 minutes)
Share the above story with your students and families. Ask: "What is so sweet about learning?" Each family discusses this question and comes up with its own answers.

Ready, Set, Mensch! Lesson 3
Essential Question: How can we practice *talmud Torah* in our own lives?

Lesson Objectives: Students will be able to:
1. Provide concrete examples of ways to practice *talmud Torah* in our own lives.
2. Describe the people—teachers, parents, friends, study partners—who help them learn best.
3. Understand how teaching helps you learn.

Getting Started: (5 minutes)
Point to the **photo of students** (page 69). A volunteer reads the caption aloud. Ask each student to think about one goal he or she has for the future and what he or she must learn in order to achieve that goal. Ask: "Is there anything that may get in the way of you doing that learning?" (*I watch TV instead, my friend calls and we decide to go to the mall.*) Have students suggest tips about how to make sure they stay on track and learn what they must learn to achieve their goals. Explain that in this class we will talk about many tips to help us learn better.

Exploring the Text:
1. (8 minutes) Students complete **Follow the Leader** (page 72) individually. Once they've completed their lists, each student chooses the description he or she considers the most important. Students share their answers with the class and explain why they chose that description. List the different descriptions on the board.
2. (7 minutes) Students complete **Study with a Buddy** (page 72) and share their answers with a partner. Discuss: How can friends and study companions also be teachers? Tell your class that later in the book we'll spend a whole chapter describing how to be a good friend.
3. (5 minutes) Students complete **Setting Aside Time** (page 73). Students may add additional hours—either before 3 p.m. or after 8 p.m—in the green space around the time chart. Congratulate them on the learning they are doing, and encourage them to do more.
4. (5 minutes) Students complete **Learn for Fun** (page 73). Vote on the class's favorite subject.
5. **Experiential Learning:** (15 minutes) Each student presents a 2-minute lesson on the subject of his or her choice. (*Suggest: How to play an instrument, a sport, or a video game.*) Do as many presentations as time allows. After each presentation, ask the rest of the class: "What did you learn?" Ask the student: "What did you learn from teaching?" After all the presentations, point out how much the class learned in a short period of time. Who knows? Perhaps the exercise will inspire future teachers. Read page 72 together.

Wrapping It Up: (5 minutes)
Each person has different ways he or she learns best. Each student completes the sentence, "I learn best when I _____."

A Kid's Mensch Handbook • Teacher's Lesson Plan Manual

Be a Mensch to Your Family, Lesson 1
Essential Question: What does the value of *sh'lom bayit* teach us?

Lesson Objectives: Students will be able to:
1. Define *sh'lom bayit*.
2. Explain why *sh'lom bayit* is important.
3. Provide examples of ways to create *sh'lom bayit*.

Getting Started: (5 minutes)
Students complete the following sentence silently, in their heads or on a sheet of paper: "My favorite family memories are _____." Students share their memories with the class. Ask: "What made the events or moments special? How were members of your family menschen to one another at the time?" Explain that in this chapter, we'll learn about *sh'lom bayit*, the mitzvah that can help us to create positive, happy memories every day.

Exploring the Text:
1. (5 minutes) Read the first paragraph of **The Family Mensch** (page 77) aloud. Students stand up any time someone makes a bad choice, and explain what that person should have done differently. Point out that all the members of the family—Jacob, Joseph, and the brothers—made choices that contributed to their difficult family life. Finish reading page 77.

2. (10 minutes) Students complete **Home Sweet Home** (page 78) individually. Students share with a partner one thing that they wrote that they hadn't thought about before. Be aware that students may be experiencing difficult family situations, including divorce and death. Be sensitive to your students' reactions and emotions. If a student prefers not to share, please respect his or her privacy.

3. **Experiential Learning:** (10 minutes) Each student creates a "family paper chain." Provide the class with light-colored construction paper, scissors, markers, and staplers. Students cut the construction paper into strips. Each student writes his or her own name on one strip of paper, and then writes the names of close family members on other strips, using one strip for each person. Students write adjectives that describe each person on each strip, and then staple their strips into chains. Each student shares his or her chains with a partner.

4. (10 minutes) Read **Shalom at Home** (page 79) together. Divide the students into groups of four. Ask each group to make a list of ways to create a peaceful home. *(Answers may include: Helping around the house; sharing with siblings; doing nice things for our parents.)* Each group shares its list, making sure not to repeat anything already said.

5. **The Tech Connection:** (5 minutes) Add *sh'lom bayit* to your class website. Post photos of students and their families together, illustrating moments of *sh'lom bayit* (*a student reading a story to her little sister, a student hugging his mom, a family sharing a festive meal together.*)

Wrapping It Up: (5 minutes)
Complete **Mensch Cake Recipe** (page 80) individually. Discuss: What do you think is the most important ingredient for *sh'lom bayit*? Why? As a class, vote on the most important ingredient. Tell your students that home is the ideal place to practice The Golden Rule—*v'ahavta l'reacha kamocha*—love your neighbor as yourself.

Be a Mensch to Your Family, Lesson 2
Essential Question: Why is respect for parents and siblings essential for a peaceful home?

Lesson Objectives: Students will be able to:
1. Discuss why respect for parents and siblings is essential for a peaceful home.
2. Explain why when we honor our parents we are also honoring God.
3. Identify strategies for how to handle conflicts with parents and siblings like a mensch.

Getting Started: (5 minutes)
Read the following quote from Rabbi Shimon bar Yoḥai to your class: "The most difficult of all *mitzvot* is 'Honor your father and mother.'" Ask: "What do you think he meant by this?"

Exploring the Text:
1. (10 minutes) Write the Ten Commandments on the board or post them in the classroom:

    Tablet 1:
    1. I am Adonai your God who brought you out of Egypt.
    2. Do not have any other gods besides Me or pray to idols.
    3. Do not use My name except for holy purposes.
    4. Remember Shabbat and keep it holy.
    5. Honor your father and mother.

    Tablet 2:
    6. Do not murder.
    7. Do not commit adultery.
    8. Do not steal.
    9. Do not swear falsely.
    10. Do not desire what belongs to your neighbor.

    Ask: "What do the commandments on the first tablet have in common? What do the commandments on the second tablet have in common? Are any of the commandments out of place?" Then read **Mom and Dad: Partners in Creation** (page 81) together. Remind the students that "Honor your father and mother" applies whether you live with both your biological parents, a single parent, adoptive parents, grandparents, two dads, etc.

2. **Experiential Learning:** (10 minutes) Point to the **photo** on page 81. A student reads the caption aloud. Ask: "What are some gifts a parent can give to a child?" Encourage your students to describe gifts that are not material, such as a sense of honesty, fair play, or a connection to their Jewish heritage. Then hand out paper and markers. Each student makes a card for his or her parents thanking them for the specific gifts they have given him or her.

3. (10 minutes) Read **Brothers and Sisters: Friends for Life** (page 82) together. Students debate in pairs the question in **Mensch-Wise** (page 82). Assign each person in the pair one side of the argument. Then ask them to switch.

4. (5 minutes) Read page 83 together. Students think of ways to strengthen *sh'lom bayit* between siblings. Write their ideas on the board.

5. (5 minutes) Read **A Note of Middot** (page 87) together. Students share examples of pet peeves, such as siblings who enter their rooms without asking, or having to wash the dishes. Then their classmates suggest positive ways to apply patience to the situation, such as speaking calmly and listening to the other person.

Wrapping It Up: (5 minutes)
Ask: "When you find yourself about to say or do something hurtful to a parent or sibling, what are your best strategies to stop yourself?"

Be a Mensch to Your Family, Lesson 3
Essential Question: How can I help my family create *sh'lom bayit*?

Lesson Objectives: Students will be able to:
1. Make choices that help preserve *sh'lom bayit* in their own families.
2. Explain how positive time together as a family helps to strengthen family peace.
3. Describe the relationship between respecting themselves and respecting their families.

Getting Started: (10 minutes)
Students act out the following scenarios. In each case, one student plays the child, and the other the parent. First, act out how a child would respond who doesn't care about *sh'lom bayit*. Then, act out how a child who always wants to preserve *sh'lom bayit* would respond.

- A friend invites you to the movies. Your parent wants you to stay home, because your aunt is visiting from Australia.
- You want to adopt a puppy. Your parent is concerned that you will lose interest in it.
- Your parent won't let you wear your favorite T-shirt to Shabbat dinner.
- Explain that in this class we are going to discuss practical ways that we can create *sh'lom bayit* in our own families.

Exploring the Text:
1. (10 minutes) Students complete **Always Speak Respectfully to Mom and Dad** (page 84) and **Be a Team Player** (page 85) individually. Each student shares his or her answers with a partner.
2. **Experiential Learning:** (15 minutes) Students complete **Do Fun Family Stuff** (page 85). Distribute markers and sheets of paper to allow students more room to record their favorite Jewish family memories. Students form small groups and each shares his or her picture with the group. Discuss: How does spending time together as a family doing fun and meaningful things help strengthen *sh'lom bayit*?
3. (5 minutes) Complete **Forgive and Forget** (page 86). Ask: "Which do you think is harder—forgiving or apologizing?" Tell your students that both involve courage and compromise—and both strengthen *sh'lom bayit*.
4. (5 minutes) Say: "Imagine that a family friend calls you a mensch in front of your parents. How do you think your parents feel? How do you feel?" Tell your students that a great way to strengthen *sh'lom bayit* is by being a mensch at home and away from home! Students complete **Be a Family Rep** (page 87).

Wrapping It Up: (5 minutes)
Make a list of family "rules" on the board that help preserve *sh'lom bayit*, such as no yelling, no name-calling, and help promptly when asked. Ask: "Which is the most difficult of these rules for you to follow?" Each student resolves to keep one of these rules that is particularly difficult for him or her for at least one week.

Be a Mensch to Your Friends and Classmates, Lesson 1

Essential Question: What makes a good friend?

Lesson Objectives: Students will be able to:
1. Understand why friendship is an important Jewish value.
2. Identify qualities to look for in a friend.
3. Explain the importance of respect, trust, and honesty in our interactions with friends and classmates.

Getting Started: (5 minutes)
Ask: "Think of one your best friends. What do you like about him or her?" Explain that in this class, we will talk about what makes a good friend.

Exploring the Text:
1. (5 minutes) Ask: "How do you decide whom to elect class president? What do you look for?" Then read **Superfriend** (page 89) together. Ask: "How is Rachel a mensch through taking action?" *(She makes students feel welcome and accepted; she sticks up for people who are being picked on; she starts school clubs.)*
2. (5 minutes) Pick a volunteer to read **Quick Quote** (page 89) aloud. Ask: "Why is it 'heroic' to turn an enemy into a friend?" *(Because it requires more effort—and courage—to make a friend of a rival or a former friend.)*
3. (10 minutes) Students answer the top of **Mensch-o-Meter** (page 90) and compare their answers with a partner. Then they complete the **exercise** on the bottom of page 90 individually.
4. (5 minutes) Read **Friend for Sale** (page 91) together. Ask: "What are some examples of nonmaterial gifts that we can give to friends?" *(Answers may include companionship, comfort, guidance, or praise.)* After reading each bulleted item, invite students to share examples of ways they made or strengthened a friendship through loyalty, honesty, or attention.
5. **Experiential Learning:** (15 minutes) Students work together, as a class or in small groups, to create a new holiday: *Yom Ḥaverim* (Friendship Day). Students must:
   - Choose a date for the new holiday.
   - Describe games or activities for the holiday.
   - Choose a theme song for the holiday (either an existing song, or an original composition).
   - Explain the importance of the holiday.
   - Create a flyer announcing the new holiday.

   Rather than assigning specific tasks, instruct students to complete the exercise through teamwork. After they've completed the exercise, the class presents the new holiday to you. Ask: "What did the exercise teach you about cooperation? What must people do in order to cooperate? What must they *not* do?"

   Read **A Note of Middot** (page 99) together. Explain that cooperating is an important part of being a good friend.

Wrapping It Up: (5 minutes)
A volunteer reads the **photo caption** on page 91 aloud. Students complete Joseph Zabara's quote in their own way: "Friendship is like _____." Students write their answers, and then use the sentence as the first line of a poem.

Be a Mensch to Your Friends and Classmates, Lesson 2

Essential Question: What is *dibbuk ḥaverim* and why is it important?

Lesson Objectives: Students will be able to:
1. Define *dibbuk ḥaverim* and explain why it is important.
2. Provide concrete examples of ways to fulfill *dibbuk ḥaverim*.
3. Describe how friendship can help us become better people.

Getting Started: (5 minutes)
Students share times when they went the extra mile to do something nice for a friend. Explain that in all those situations, the students were fulfilling the mitzvah of *dibbuk ḥaverim*—attachment to friends.

Exploring the Text:
1. **The Tech Connection:** (8 minutes) Read **A Treasure** (page 92) together. Then add *dibbuk ḥaverim* to the class website and post photos of students in the class fulfilling *dibbuk ḥaverim* (*having fun with friends, celebrating a birthday, helping a friend*).

2. (5 minutes) Read **Win-Win** (pages 93–94) together. Ask students to think about a time when friends corrected them. How did they feel? Give students a few minutes to record this memory in **A Friend Indeed** (page 94).

3. (10 minutes) Ask: "Why is it hard to criticize or correct a friend?" (*The friend may get angry at you or refuse to listen.*) Two students perform the following scenario:

    > Brian tells his friend Sara mean gossip about someone else in the class. Sara thinks it is wrong to spread mean gossip. How should Sara correct Brian so that Brian will be more likely to listen to her and actually change his ways? How does Brian respond?

    After the two students perform the scenario, discuss: How did Sara correct Brian? What did she do well? What could she have done better? If time allows, other student pairs can perform the same scenario but correct Brian in a different way.

4. (5 minutes) Point out to the students that in class, at different times we learn individually, with a partner, in a small group, or as an entire class. Ask: "How do you learn best?" Students complete **Mensch-Wise** (page 93) individually.

5. **Experiential Learning:** (12 minutes) Create a "*Dibbuk Ḥaverim* Declaration." Using markers and poster paper, your students will write: "We, the members of [name of teacher or class] hereby pledge to _____." Students create a list of ways to be good friends or classmates, with illustrations.

Wrapping It Up: (5 minutes)
Each student chooses one of the items on the list in the declaration to work on in the next week and shares his or her resolution with the class. Then the entire class signs the declaration. Hang the "*Dibbuk Ḥaverim* Declaration" in a visible place in your classroom.

Be a Mensch to Your Friends and Classmates, Lesson 3

Essential Question: How can we practice *dibbuk ḥaverim* in our own lives?

Lesson Objectives: Students will be able to:
1. Give examples of how they can practice *dibbuk ḥaverim* in their own lives.
2. Define *l'shon hara* and evaluate whether a statement is *l'shon hara*.
3. Define *kavanah* and explain why it is important for being a good friend.

Getting Started: (5 minutes)
Write on the board: "Friendship is like a bank; you cannot take from it more than you put in." Students share examples from their own lives that illustrate this point.

Exploring the Text:
1. (10 minutes) Students complete **Meet in the Middle** (page 96) together with a partner. Ask: "Are there times that a mensch should *not* compromise? What are they?"

2. (10 minutes) Tell your students: "Become more sensitive to *l'shon hara*—gossip. Before making a statement about someone, ask yourself these three questions:
   a) Is it true?
   b) Is it well meaning?
   c) Is it unlikely to hurt or insult someone?"

   If a statement doesn't receive a "yes" to all three questions—best not to say it.

   Give the class the following scenarios. Students assess whether these statements are *l'shon hara*:
   - David is sitting next to Ben and notices that he got a 100 on his science test. He tells Lisa about Ben's grade on the test.
   - Jenny tells Rachel that Becky's parents are getting a divorce. Jenny and Rachel discuss how they can help their friend get through this difficult time.
   - Zack is thinking about whether to join the basketball team. He asks his friend Dan, who is already on the team, what he thinks about the coach. Dan does not like the coach very much, but he really wants Zack to join the team. So Dan tells Zack that the coach pushes them hard (which is true), but he doesn't tell him that the coach sometimes insults them.

3. (10 minutes) Students act out two scenarios: One in which one person speaks and the other listens with *kavanah*—concentration—and one in which one person speaks and the other looks around, whistles, or looks at his or her watch. Ask the class: "Why is it important for a mensch to be a good listener?"

4. **Experiential Learning:** (10 minutes) Read **Be Grateful for Your Friends** (page 98), and students share their answers with the class. Teach the class Debbie Friedman's "Sheheheyanu" and sing together. You can download the song at http://itunes.apple.com/au/album/and-youth-shall-see-visions/id77723454.

Wrapping It Up: (5 minutes)
Going around the room, each student says to the person next to him or her, "You are a good friend because_____." Then the person says, "I will be an even better friend by _____." Make sure to give specific, concrete ways that each student is a good friend and can become a better friend.

Be a Mensch to Everyone, Lesson 1

Essential Question: How does performing *mitzvot* and respecting others help repair the world?

Lesson Objectives: Students will be able to:
1. Define *tikkun olam*.
2. Explain how every mitzvah helps to repair the world.
3. Define *k'vod hab'riyot* and provide examples.

Getting Started: (5 minutes)
Read aloud this quote from the chapter: "I always give much away, and so gather happiness instead of pleasure." Illustrate the difference between happiness and pleasure in this way:

- Students describe the *pleasure* they experience when eating their favorite dinner.
- Then they describe the *happiness* they experience when delivering dinner to a needy family.

Students provide additional examples of the difference between happiness and pleasure. Explain that this chapter will be about the happiness we feel and create through being a mensch.

Exploring the Text:
1. (5 minutes) Read page 101 together. According to Rabbi Isaac Luria, how can each person help to repair the world?

2. (10 minutes) Read Rabbi Baruch of Medziboz's **quote** on page 101 aloud. Ask: "Why is every single person necessary to repair the world?" Explain that according to the Jewish tradition, each person has a job that only he or she can do to repair the world. Divide the students into small groups, and each group brainstorms different kinds of jobs. Examples may include:

    - Choosing a career that helps others, such as medicine or education. Explain that we can bring generosity and kindness to many professions.
    - Having a positive effect on others by being cheerful or helping people through their problems.
    - Being helpful at home and in the community.

3. (10 minutes) Students complete **Repairing the World** (page 102) individually and then each shares answers with a partner.

4. **The Tech Connection:** (5 minutes) Read page 103 together, and add *k'vod hab'riyot* to your class website. Illustrate with images of people from different countries, races, religions, and cultures.

5. **Experiential Learning:** (10 minutes) Read **The Kavod Railroad** (page 104) together. To illustrate the "contagious" quality of *kavod*, bring dominoes to class. Stand one domino on a large table or on the floor and say: "I place a dollar in the *tzedakah* box." Invite students to continue the story by placing additional dominoes, one next to the other, to represent the next steps. (*Examples include: The dollar goes toward curing a disease; one child who was ill is now cured; she grows up to be a doctor; etc.*) Once the class has exhausted its ideas (or dominoes), tip the first domino and watch the "Kavod Railroad" go!

Wrapping It Up: (5 minutes)
Each student answers the questions on the bottom of page 104. Ask: "How does *k'vod hab'riyot* help repair the world?"

Be a Mensch to Everyone, Lesson 2

Essential Question: How can I practice respect for others in my everyday interactions and through giving *tzedakah*?

Lesson Objectives: Students will be able to:
1. Identify ways of practicing respect for others in their own lives.
2. Define *derech eretz* and provide examples.
3. Define *tzedakah* and discuss conflicting priorities in giving *tzedakah*.

Getting Started: (5 minutes)
Divide the students into groups of two or three. Each group lists as many ways as possible that it can practice respect in everyday interactions. See who can list the most ways in 3 minutes. When the groups are done, explain that Jewish tradition calls this everyday respect *derech eretz*. Explain that in this class, we will learn about different ways to practice respect for others, both on an everyday basis and on special occasions.

Exploring the Text:
1. (5 minutes) Read **Derech Eretz: The Mensch Way** (page 105) together, and each student completes **Mensch Manners** (page 106) individually. Students share their resolutions with the class.

2. (5 minutes) Read **Tzedakah: The Right Thing** (page 110) together. Review the first paragraph by asking: "What is the difference between charity and *tzedakah*?"

3. (10 minutes) Divide the students into small groups. Give each group eight index cards, with one of Maimonides' eight levels written on each card. Each group must arrange the cards in order of least praise-worthy to most praise-worthy (without looking at Maimonides' order), and label the cards one through eight, with one being the least praise-worthy and eight being the most praise-worthy. Each group explains why it chose the order of the cards. Then look at **Maimonides' order** on page 111. Why did he choose the order he did?

4. **Experiential Learning:** (15 minutes) Choose and plan a class *tzedakah* project. You may have to give some students assignments to work on outside of class. Ideas include:
   - Make a class *tzedakah* box, collect money each class, and vote on a *tzedakah* recipient.
   - Make a canned food drive for a local food pantry. Create flyers to post around the school publicizing the drive, and a send note home to parents requesting them to bring in cans.
   - Plan a "make your own ice-cream sundae" sale during the break at school. Buy ice cream, hot fudge, candy, etc. and sell to the other students in the school. All proceeds go to the *tzedakah* recipient the class chooses.

5. **The Tech Connection:** (5 minutes) Students research potential *tzedakah* recipients on the Internet and gather information about each one in order to convince their classmates that this is a worthy cause.

> **Wrapping It Up:** (5 minutes)
> Reflect on the process of planning the *tzedakah* project. What criteria did you use to choose a *tzedakah* recipient and what to give them? Was it important to you whether the recipient was Jewish or not? Local or not? Will the *tzedakah* help that person become self-sufficient? Point out the complexity and conflicting values in choosing how to fulfill the mitzvah of *tzedakah*.

Be a Mensch to Everyone, Lesson 3
Essential Question: What can I do to support the Jewish community?

Lesson Objectives: Students will be able to:
1. Define *k'lal Yisrael*.
2. Explain why all Jews are responsible for each other.
3. Provide concrete examples of ways to support *k'lal Yisrael*.

Getting Started: (5 minutes)
Ask: "Which do you most identify as: Jewish, American, human, or a member of your family?" Students stand up and go to one of the four corners of the room, where each corner represents one of the above categories. Ask representatives from each corner to explain why they chose their corner. Explain that we have many conflicting identities and responsibilities, and we belong to many different communities. We already discussed *k'vod hab'riyot*, our obligation to respect all humans. Now we are going to focus on our responsibilities to *k'lal Yisrael*, the Jewish community.

Exploring the Text:
1. (5 minutes) Read **K'lal Yisrael: One Big Family** (page 107). Ask: "In what ways is *k'lal Yisrael*—the world Jewish community—like one big family?" *(Answers may include: We share the same homeland—Israel; we respect one another; we are responsible for one another; it is important to stick together, even though we may disagree.)*

2. (5 minutes) Read together the **list** on page 108. Then have students brainstorm more ways to support the Jewish community.

3. **Experiential Learning:** (15 minutes) Celebrate Israel in your classroom. Bring in pita and hummus, play CDs of Israeli music, or invite an Israeli dance teacher to your class to teach a few steps. If possible, welcome an Israeli (teens are best!) to speak to your class about life in Israel. Help your students to see that their lives are similar to those of Israeli kids: They like to play video games, talk on the phone, watch TV, and use e-mail, too! Encourage the students to use as many Hebrew words and phrases as they can in the classroom. When students enter the room, say *shalom*; when they leave, say *l'hitra'ot*—see you later!

4. (5 minutes) Read **Mensch Spotlight** (page 109) together. Ask: "In what way did *k'lal Yisrael* and *k'vod hab'riyot* influence Henrietta Szold's actions? *(She worked not only to help Jews but Arabs of Palestine as well.)*

5. **The Tech Connection:** (10 minutes) Each student chooses a mensch who, like Henrietta Szold, worked hard to help *k'lal Yisrael*. Each student researches the person on the Internet and writes a brief paragraph about him or her. Post the students' paragraphs on the class website.

Wrapping It Up: (5 minutes)
Each student chooses one new way he or she would like to support the Jewish community and shares it with the class.

Assessments

You can assess your students' work in a wide variety of ways:

1. Read **Mensch Magic** on pages 112-113 together. Each student writes a reflection on the following three questions:
   - For you, what was the most memorable lesson in *A Kid's Mensch Handbook*?
   - What new ways to be a mensch did you learn in *A Kid's Mensch Handbook*?
   - How do you plan to make your own "mensch-ful splash"?

2. Each student completes a **Mensch Diploma** (pages 114-115). Then collect the books and fill in the date and name lines. Congratulate your students on completing the book and on acquiring valuable knowledge from our Jewish ancestors, one another, and themselves.

   If possible, plan a ceremony to which you may invite parents, your principal, rabbi, cantor, or any other special guests. Then, one at a time, call each of your students up to the front of the class to receive his or her book with the completed certificate. Each student shares his or her answer to the question above: How do you plan to make your own "mensch-ful splash"? Prepare your students by asking them to write out what they would like to say in advance. You may also wish to compose a short speech for each student, specifying a particular way that student was a mensch. For example, "For Rebecca, who always listened carefully to her classmates and asked good questions."

3. Use the **Index** (pages 116–118) to review the book. The students in the class divide the questions so that each student (or pair of students) has four or five questions to answer. Each student (or pair) presents his or her answers to the class, and/or posts the answers on the class website.

4. Students present a skit, write a song, or create a presentation on the computer exploring one of the Jewish values they learned about in this book. The project should include concrete examples—real or imaginary—of people practicing these values.

5. Individually, in pairs, or in small groups, the students create their very own mensch projects. Projects may include:
   - Teach a class of younger students about basic ways to stay healthy and take care of their bodies.
   - Research your family's history, by interviewing your parents, grandparents, or other family members to find out about your family's stories and values.
   - Plan a car wash, bake sale, make your own ice-cream sale, etc. to raise money for the *tzedakah* recipient of your choice.
   - Volunteer at a local soup kitchen or nursing home.
   - Organize a Jewish holiday party for the younger children in your community.
   - Form a New Kid Welcoming Committee for your school.

   Encourage your students to be creative and work together in making their own "mensch-ful splash."

www.ingramcontent.com/pod-product-compliance
Lightning Source LLC
Chambersburg PA
CBHW081220230426
43666CB00015B/2827